The Last Lighthouse Keeper

Written by Matilda May

Illustrated by Chantal Stewart

Flying Start
to Literacy®

Contents

Chapter 1:
Time to move on

Jenny's mum and dad were the lightkeepers for the oldest lighthouse in the country. They had lived on Rocky Island for as long as she could remember.

And for as long as she could remember, every night her Dad had lit the lamp in the old lighthouse and stayed up all night to make sure it did not go out.

But everything was about to change.
This weekend, they would say goodbye to
the old lighthouse and the island. There was
a new electric light tower, and tomorrow
it would be turned on for the first time.

"I can't believe that tonight will be the last
time you light the lamp," said Jenny.

Jenny and her mum made a cake shaped like a lighthouse to celebrate their last night.

Her mum and dad looked a bit sad. Jenny was sad too, but she was also excited, because they were going to live in a big town. She could not wait to go to a big school and make lots of friends.

"Come on," said Mum. "This is a special
night. Let's go and light the lamp. We can
take the cake with us."

Together, they climbed the ninety-six stairs up to the lamp room. Jenny watched her dad light the lamp. Then he cranked up the machine that would slowly turn the light all night.

They watched the light beam flash slowly over the sea while they ate cake. The light warned the ships to stay away from the rocky coast. For one last night, this light would keep the ships safe.

When it was time for bed, Jenny and her mum said goodnight to Dad. He would have to stay up all night to look after the light for the last time.

Chapter 2:
The new light

The next morning, Jenny went to the lighthouse to help her dad. She took her camera so she could take photos of Dad in the lamp room for the last time.

As they looked out to sea, they could see dark storm clouds.

"This storm will be a good test for the new electric light," said Jenny's dad.

"I hope it's a huge storm," said Jenny, who loved watching the sky flash with lightning.

"We'd better turn on the new light tower now," said Dad.

They closed up the old lighthouse and walked over to the new light tower. Dad turned on the engine, and the light in the new light tower began to shine and flash.

"It's not as pretty as our lighthouse," said Jenny sadly.

Then there was a drop of rain and strong
gusts of wind. The ocean roared beneath
the cliffs, and waves crashed. The rain
began to come faster.

"Quick, Jenny, let's go inside," said Dad.

"Where's my camera?" said Jenny.

"You must have left it in the old lighthouse," said Dad.

"I'll be back in a minute," said Jenny.

"Hurry," said Dad.

Jenny raced back to the old lighthouse and
quickly climbed up the stairs. Just as
she reached the lamp room, she heard
a loud bang.

A huge gust of wind had slammed shut the
heavy steel door.

Jenny ran down the stairs. She could not open the door – she was locked in!

She banged on the door.

"Dad, Dad, help! I can't open the door!" she shouted.

She could hear Dad outside in the storm. He was shaking the door, but it wouldn't open.

"The lock has broken, Jen. I can't open it," shouted Dad, through the thick metal door.

Just then, Jenny heard another loud bang.

"Dad, what was that noise? What happened?" asked Jenny.

"It's the new light tower. It's been hit by lightning," said Dad. "The light has stopped working."

Chapter 3:
An old light

The storm raged outside the lighthouse. Jenny could hear her mother shouting on the other side of the door.

"Jenny, you will have to light the lamp," she shouted. "There needs to be a light for the ships in this storm."

It was dark inside the lighthouse. Jenny
turned on the torch by the door. She
climbed the stairs quickly to the lamp room.

Raindrops splashed onto the glass dome,
and lightning flashed across the black sky.
It was a great storm, but Jenny tried not to
watch. She had to concentrate. She had
watched Dad light the lamp a hundred
times – would she be able to do it now?

Jenny lit the lamp carefully. Then she cranked up the machine, and the light began to turn slowly.

Jenny sat down and watched the storm. It would be the last storm she would see in the old lighthouse.

She sat up all night, making sure the light stayed lit and the machine kept turning. Finally, as the sun started to rise, she fell asleep.

Chapter 4:
The last lighthouse keeper

A kiss on the cheek woke up Jenny.
She opened her eyes and saw her parents
smiling down at her.

"Wakey, wakey, lightkeeper," said Mum.

Jenny looked around. The sun was shining.
The storm was over.

"You got the door open. That took ages!" said Jenny, stretching and yawning.

"Well done, Jenny, you kept the light on all night. Without you, a ship might have crashed on the rocks," said Dad.

"Does that mean I'm the last lightkeeper on Rocky Island?" asked Jenny.

"Yes, I think you are!" said Dad.

Appendix: Lightkeepers

In the past, lighthouses had lightkeepers. A lightkeeper made sure that the light, the lense and all the parts of the lighthouse worked properly. The lightkeeper had to turn on, or light, the lamp every evening at sunset and turn it off at sunrise.

Each lighthouse had at least two lightkeepers – a head lightkeeper and one or more assistant lightkeepers. If one lightkeeper was ill or injured, there was always another lightkeeper who could light the lamp each evening.

Today, most lighthouses run on electricity and are automatic. Some lighthouses still have keepers who make weather reports and rescue people in an emergency.